EDGE
BOOKS™

TOP SECRET FILES

SECRETS OF WORLD WAR I

BY SEAN McCOLLUM

CAPSTONE PRESS
a capstone imprint

Edge Books are published by Capstone Press,
1710 Roe Crest Drive, North Mankato, Minnesota 56003
www.mycapstone.com

Copyright © 2017 by Capstone Press, a Capstone imprint. All rights reserved. No part of
this publication may be reproduced in whole or in part, or stored in a retrieval system, or
transmitted in any form or by any means, electronic, mechanical, photocopying,
recording, or otherwise, without written permission of the publisher.

Library of Congress Cataloging-in-Publication Data
Library of Congress Catalog-in-Publication Data
is on file with the Library of Congress.

Editorial Credits
Nate LeBoutillier, editor; Steve Mead, designer;
Pam Mitsakos, media researcher, Laura Manthe, production specialist

Photo Credits
Alamy: Arterra Picture Library, 23, Everett Collection Historical, 10; Bridgeman Images:
UIG/Underwood Archives, 18-19; Getty Images: Bettmann, 15, 26, DEA/A. DAGLI ORT, 5,
Hulton Archive, 11; Newscom: Ann Ronan Picture Library Heritage Images, 21, The Print
Collector Heritage Images, 24, Tim Barker KRT, 29; Shutterstock: Eugene Sergeev, 22,
Everett Historical, cover, 2-3 background, 7, 8, 9 13, 16, 17, 18 top left, 27, 28, Olemac,
25 bottom middle; Thinkstock: Peter Davies, 25 top right

Shutterstock: Design Elements, Everett Historical, Davor Ratkovic, javarman, STILLFX

Printed and bound in China.
007891

TABLE OF CONTENTS

THE BLACK HAND LIGHTS THE FUSE

Gavrilo Princip, 19, stepped off a curb in Sarajevo and aimed his pistol. His target was the Archduke Franz Ferdinand. Ferdinand was in line to become Austria-Hungary's next emperor. Young Princip belonged to the Black Hand, a secret terrorist group. The Black Hand hoped to drive out the ruling Austro-Hungarian Empire and unite all Serbian people. As Ferdinand's open car drove past, Princip jumped at his chance. With two shots he killed both the Archduke and his wife. The date was June 28, 1914.

The murders were like a match lighting the fuse of a huge bomb. Austria-Hungary declared war on Serbia a month later. Other countries soon joined the conflict. Before long, most of Europe, and later other countries across the globe, marched into the Great War.

EARLIER ATTEMPT

Archduke Ferdinand survived an **assassination** attempt earlier in the day on June 28, 1914. A different Black Hand terrorist attempted to throw a grenade into Ferdinand's car, but it bounced off. The explosion wounded up to 20 other people. After giving a speech, Ferdinand was headed to the hospital with his wife, Sophie, to visit the injured when they were killed.

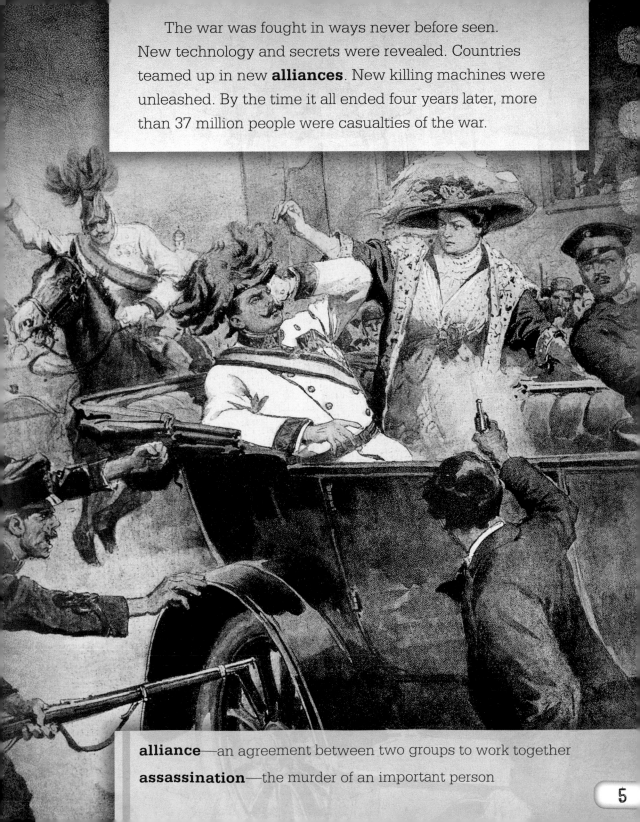

The war was fought in ways never before seen. New technology and secrets were revealed. Countries teamed up in new **alliances**. New killing machines were unleashed. By the time it all ended four years later, more than 37 million people were casualties of the war.

alliance—an agreement between two groups to work together

assassination—the murder of an important person

CHAPTER ONE

SECRET PLANS, SECRET PLOTS

THE CENTRAL POWERS

World War I started on July 28, 1914. On that date Austria-Hungary declared war on Serbia. The invasion that followed set in motion a series of alliances.

Powerful Germany allied itself with Austria-Hungary. This honored an agreement the two had signed in 1879. Right after the war began, Germany also signed a secret **treaty** with the **Ottoman Empire**. About a year later, Bulgaria joined the alliance. Germany secretly promised these allies territory if they won.

THE ALLIED POWERS

Austria-Hungary's invasion of Serbia triggered alliances on the other side, too. Russia, Serbia's supporter, prepared for war. France had a treaty to aid Russia if it was attacked. Great Britain and its colonies joined the cause after Germany invaded its ally, Belgium. Both sides raced toward the battlefield. Many people thought the fighting would be over by the end of 1914. They were very, very wrong.

FAMILY FEUD

World War I was a family feud in some ways. Royal families across Europe had intermarried. A number of World War I's leaders were therefore related. Germany's Kaiser Wilhelm II, King George V of England, and the Russian Czar Nicholas II were cousins. Only England's King George V would still be king once the war ended.

Side by side, Czar Nicholas II (back seat, dark hat) and Kaiser Wilhelm II enjoy a pre-war carriage ride.

treaty—official agreement between two or more countries

Ottoman Empire—state created by Turkish tribes that peaked during the 15th and 16th century

GERMANY'S SURPRISE ATTACK

German leaders believed they had a secret strategy that promised swift victory. Years before the war, their generals had drawn up the Schlieffen plan for a surprise attack. First, German armies would conquer France. Second, they would turn eastward and strike Russia.

In August 1914, Germany launched the attack. Its forces shocked everyone by illegally pushing through Belgium, a **neutral** country, in order to invade France. However, French forces stopped the German advance at the First Battle of the Marne.

German machine gunning crew

THE SECRET TREATY OF LONDON

Not all countries honored their pre-war treaties. Before the war, Italy was an ally of Germany and Austria-Hungary. But it refused to join the Central Powers once war was declared. Instead, Italy's leaders started secret negotiations with Britain, France, and Russia. In 1915, they signed the Treaty of London. They declared war on Austria-Hungary that year and Germany in 1916. In return, they were secretly promised territory if the Allies won.

✓ Taxis in Paris form a line to take soldiers to the war.

FIGHTING FACT The French Army hired about 600 Paris taxis to rush 6,000 soldiers to the Battle of the Marne.

neutral—not supporting or agreeing with either side of a disagreement or competition

GERMANY'S SECRET PLOTS

By 1916, neither side was gaining ground. Germany launched two secret plots to try to change the game in its favor.

THE ZIMMERMAN TELEGRAM

German officials feared the United States might join the Allied Powers. In a secret message in January 1917, German officials urged Mexico to invade the U.S. to tie up the U.S. military. British agents, however, intercepted the message, known as the Zimmerman Telegram. They decoded it and passed it to U.S. officials. The contents angered many Americans who had hoped the U.S. would stay out of the war. It contributed to the U.S. declaring war on Germany in April 1917.

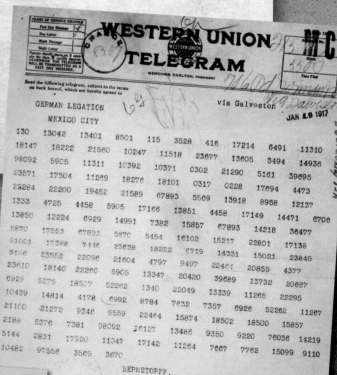

Zimmerman Telegram ↗

MAJOR ALLIED POWERS	CENTRAL POWERS
France	Germany
Great Britain (and its colonies)	Austria-Hungary
Russia (1914–1917)	Ottoman Empire
Serbia	Bulgaria (1915–1918)
Japan	
Italy (1915–1918)	
United States (1917–1918)	
Greece (1917–1918)	

LENIN'S SECRET TRAIN

By 1917 the war had killed millions of Russia's soldiers and caused widespread starvation in the country. Many suffering Russians turned against their government. Vladimir Lenin was a Russian revolutionary who wanted to get Russia out of the war. He had been **exiled** in Switzerland. Germany agreed to put Lenin on a secret train returning him to Russia. Germany's strategy worked as Lenin soon became a top leader of the Russian Revolution. This revolution knocked Russia out of the war just as Germany had hoped, giving them one less major opponent.

↑ Vladimir Lenin

exile—to send someone away from his or her own country, usually for political reasons

11

SECRET WEAPONS

World War I, like all wars, inspired **innovation**. Both sides invented terrible weapons to destroy the enemy. They also rushed to find ways to counter them to protect their own men.

U-BOATS

Before the war, Germany had built a fleet of modern submarines known as U-Boats. Hidden beneath the waves, they sneaked up on Allied vessels and sank them with torpedoes. They hunted warships and terrorized supply ships, too. During the war, they sank almost 5,000 Allied ships.

Q-SHIPS

To fight back against U-Boats, the British navy created top-secret Q-ships. These were gunships disguised as fishing boats or cargo ships. Submarines were supposed to warn **civilian** ships that they were about to be sunk. This gave crews time to abandon ship. Q-ship crews might send a few men off in a lifeboat. Then when the U-Boat came in for the kill, the Q-ship revealed its hidden guns and opened fire.

THE SECRET OF THE *LUSITANIA*

A German U-Boat attacked the British ocean liner RMS *Lusitania* on May 7, 1915. More than 1,000 passengers were killed, including 128 Americans. The U.S. was still neutral at the time, but the attack caused more Americans to turn against Germany. The Allies, though, did not reveal one secret. *Lusitania* was carrying military supplies as well as civilian passengers.

A German U-Boat torpedo passes the bow of the lusitania. ↓

innovation—a new idea or invention

civilian—a person who is not in the military

AERIAL BOMBING

In 1903, the first powered airplane flew. Just 11 years later, armies experimented with turning them into flying weapons. For example, World War I saw the first use of aircraft to bomb targets. Germany sent gas-filled zeppelins to attack Britain in January 1915. The raids were scary and sometimes destructive. The Brits, however, introduced explosive bullets that could shoot down the zeppelins. Soon both sides relied more on "heavy bombers." These big planes could drop more than 1,000 pounds (454 kilograms) of explosives.

FIGHTING
FACT

A zeppelin's huge gas bag was made of cow intestines. More than 250,000 cows were needed to build one of these airships.

FIGHTER PLANES

Early in the war, armies used airplanes mainly to scout enemy positions. To stop this, both sides armed their planes to shoot down enemy aircraft. This led to dogfights—duels in the sky between daredevil pilots. Manfred von Richthofen, the German fighter pilot nicknamed the Red Baron, is well-known for his many victories. The most famous American fighter ace was Eddie Rickenbacker. He was such a good mechanic that the US Army did not want him to fly. But he proved his skill in the air, downing 26 enemy aircraft.

↓ Eddie Rickenbacker

MACHINE GUNS

World War I soldiers faced firepower never before
seen on battlefields. One of the deadliest weapons was
the machine gun. They were heavy and bulky, but some
could fire 500 rounds per minute. At the Battle of the
Somme (July 1–November 18, 1916), some 58,000 British
infantry were killed or wounded on the first day. Most
were cut down by machine guns. Such new, deadly
weapons made old-fashioned infantry charges and other
tactics worse than worthless. Early in the war, both
sides dug long trench systems to protect their men.

ARTILLERY

Artillery proved the deadliest weapons of World War I. These field guns could fire shells faster, farther, and more accurately than cannons of the past. One of Germany's secret weapons was the "Paris Gun," first used in 1918. This supergun's big shells could blast the French capital from a distance of 75 miles (120 km). It had a barrel more than 110 feet (34 m) long and required a crew of 80 men. Its main purpose was to scare the people of Paris by letting them know that they could be harmed even from far away.

infantry—a group of soldiers trained to fight and travel on foot

tactic—a plan for fighting a battle

A soldier in a Russian trench uses a gas mask. →

POISON GAS

From 1915 to 1917, the frontlines moved only a few miles. The armies experimented with new weapons to try to break the **stalemate**. In 1915 the Germans attacked with chlorine gas in several battles. The gray-green clouds floated over and into enemy trenches, poisoning Allied soldiers. The Allies soon responded with gas attacks of their own. Both sides rushed to equip their men with gas masks. In 1917 the armies fired mustard gas shells at each other. This poison burned the skin and blinded the eyes. It could kill if inhaled.

stalemate—situation where neither side of opposing forces can win

TANKS

In 1916, Britain introduced a new weapon—a type of armored tractor. They were code-named "tanks," as in water tanks, to keep them secret. The first tanks surprised British troops as much as their enemies. The steel plating protected their crews from gunfire when they rolled into the dangerous area known as "No Man's Land." However, they often broke down or got stuck in mud. By the end of 1917, though, newer models proved effective in leading infantry assaults on German trenches.

FIGHTING FACT

Both sides tried flamethrowers to drive the enemy from trenches. But flamethrower squads could rarely get close enough to their target before being shot down.

↓ British tanks roll into action in 1917.

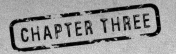

SPIES, NEW TACTICS, NEW TECH

In war, nothing is more secret than spy work. World War I saw thousands of civilians risk their lives to share important information about the enemy.

LA DAME BLANCHE

After the German invasion in 1914, the people of Belgium rapidly created a spy network. It was called La Dame Blanche, or "The White Lady." It was made up of entire families, including children. They counted German trains and reported on troop movements. The group eventually had some 1,300 agents—a third of them women—spying on the Germans. Secret messengers carried the precious information to Allied agents in neighboring Holland.

FIGHTING FACT

Marthe Cnockaert had her village ruined by German forces and so she became a spy for the Allies. Following the war she went on to write spy novels with her husband.

Edith Cavell →

SECRET AGENT NURSE

Edith Cavell was a British nurse working in Belgium when the Germans invaded. She saved the lives of many German as well as Allied soldiers. But Cavell also helped about 200 Allied prisoners escape. The Germans caught her and sentenced her to death for **espionage**. Despite international outrage, a firing squad executed her in October 1915. Her bravery became an inspiring symbol for Allied troops.

espionage—the actions of a spy to gain sensitive national, political, or economic information

INSTANT MESSAGES

During the war, communication and **intelligence** were as important as guns and bombs. Radio communication was introduced to warfare during World War I. For the first time, commanders could learn instantly what was happening and give orders. They no longer had to send a written message or string telegraph wires. Both sides also experimented with radios in aircraft. Flying scouts could then report enemy positions and movements as they happened. But this new wireless tech was sometimes unreliable. Many officers still chose homing pigeons to send important messages.

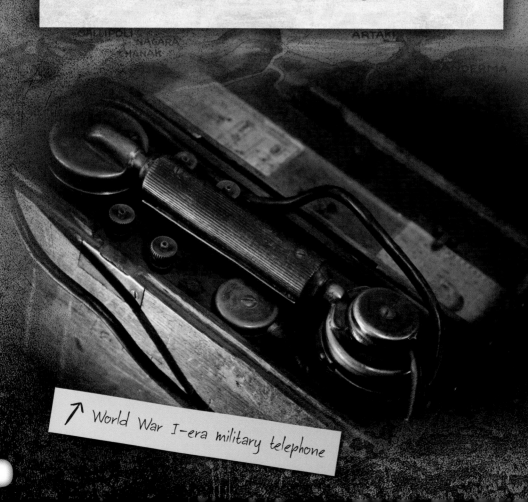

↑ World War I-era military telephone

FIGHTING FACT

In 1918, a wounded homing pigeon helped rescue 200 trapped American soldiers. Named Cher Ami—French for "dear friend"—the bird received top military honors after the war.

PUZZLE MASTERS

Top-secret intelligence teams served as key parts of the war effort. They intercepted enemy messages and collected reports from spies. They then pieced together information to figure out the enemy's next moves. Britain's "Room 40" was home to the war's best intelligence crew. These men and women cracked thousands of coded messages. One was the Zimmerman Telegram that helped convince the U.S. to go to war.

intelligence—secret information about an enemy's plans or actions

THE MINES OF MESSINES

Trench warfare forced both sides to try new tactics to win the war. British engineers dug secret tunnels toward German trenches near the French town of Messines for 18 months. They formed caves under the German trenches and packed them with 600 tons of explosives. On June 7, 1917, the Mines of Messines exploded, instantly killing about 10,000 German troops. Afterward, British and French forces easily swept forward.

FIGHTING FACT

When the Mines of Messines were set off, the explosions were heard more than 1,500 miles (2,414 km) away.

↗ British soldiers dig secret tunnels in Belgium.

ATTACK OF THE STORM BATTALIONS

In spring 1918 Germany launched a desperate drive to win the war. It used a new tactic—Storm Battalions. They divided their big armies into smaller squads that could move and attack fast. They were armed with light weapons like grenades and handheld machine guns, a new invention. The quick strikes of these Storm Battalions shocked Allied positions and drove them back. But the Central Powers were running out of men. The **offensive** stalled.

offensive—an attack by armed forces

ARABS VS. THE OTTOMAN TURKS

World War I was also fought in North Africa and the Middle East, part of the Ottoman Empire. The Allies promised independence to Arab groups there if they helped fight the Ottoman Turks. A brilliant British officer named T.E. Lawrence joined with Arab rebels. Together they staged raid after daring raid. They also captured the important port city of Aqaba. In the end, British and French officials betrayed their Arab allies. In 1916, Britain and France had signed a secret deal known as the Sykes-Picot Agreement. It sliced up the region into colonies their two countries controlled.

lawrence of Arabia →

↑ People come together to celebrate the end of The Great War.

A RACE TO THE FINISH

By late 1917 Russia quit fighting after a revolution overthrew its government. That freed German troops to shift to the Western Front. Germany hoped the added armies could break through into Paris and win the war.

The United States declared war against the Central Powers in April 1917. By spring 1918 fresh American forces were reaching the battlefields. They helped block the last big German offensive. Then they joined the Allied offensive to defeat Germany. World War I officially ended on November 11, 1918.

FIGHTING FACT

The U.S. **mobilized** 4.7 million men to fight in World War I. About 110,000 American troops died during the war—43,000 from a deadly type of flu.

mobilize—to assemble armed forces to be ready to fight

A WORLD-CHANGING WAR

World War I dramatically changed the world, especially Europe and the Middle East. Millions of young soldiers never had a chance to live, work, and raise families. Germany and Russia's royal families were overthrown. The empires of Austria-Hungary and the Ottomans were broken up. Maps from before and after the war help tell the story.

Unfortunately, post-war changes did not lead to lasting peace. Within 15 years, Germany—led by Adolf Hitler and the Nazis—began a secret military build-up. And just 21 years after the end of World War I, countries again marched toward the deadliest war ever.

↑ World War I leads directly to the formation of the Nazi Party and the more momentous World War II.

Europe after World War I

- Under League of Nations' supervision
- Areas ceded by Germany
- Demilitarized Rhine-area 1919-1936
- People vote on territory
- Russian Czar's earlier territory
- Belonged to Austria-Hungary until 1918

Finland

Estonia

Latvia

Lithuania

U.S.S.R

Sweden

Denmark

East
Prussia

Poland

Holland

Germany

Belg.

Alsace-
Lorraine

Czechoslovakia

Switz.

Austria

South
Tyrol

Hungary

France

Romania

Italy

Yugoslavia

Bulgaria

GLOSSARY

alliance (uh-LY-uhnts)—an agreement between two groups to work together

assassination (uh-SAS-uh-nay-shun)—the murder of an important person

civilian (si-VIL-yuhn)—a person who is not in the military

espionage (ESS-pee-uh-nahzh)—the actions of a spy to gain sensitive national, political, or economic information

exile (EG-zile)—to send someone away from his or her own country, usually for political reasons

infantry (IN-fuhn-tree)—a group of soldiers trained to fight and travel on foot

innovation (in-uh-VAY-shuhn)—a new idea or invention

intelligence (in-TEL-uh-jenss)—secret information about an enemy's plans or actions

mobilize (MOH-buh-lize)—to assemble armed forces to be ready to fight

neutral (NOO-truhl)—not supporting or agreeing with either side of a disagreement or competition

offensive (uh-FEN-siv)—an attack by armed forces

Ottoman Empire (AH-toh-muhn EM-pihr)—state created by Turkish tribes that peaked in the 15th and 16th centuries

stalemate (STALE-mate)—situation in which neither side of opposing forces can win

tactic (TAK-tik)—a plan for fighting a battle

treaty (TREE-tee)—an official agreement between two or more countries

CRITICAL THINKING USING THE COMMON CORE

1. Read the text on page 11. How did World War I help set the stage for the Russian Revolution? (Key Ideas and Details)

2. How did World War I change the way people fought wars? How much of a factor do you think technology played in the final outcome? (Integration of Knowledge and Ideas)

READ MORE

Adams, Simon. *World War I.* New York: DK Eyewitness Books, 2014.

Rasmussen, R. Kent. *World War I for Kids.* Chicago: Chicago Review Press, Incorporated; 2014.

Swain, Gwyneth. *World War I: An Interactive History Adventure*. Mankato, Minn: Capstone Press, 2014.

INTERNET SITES

FactHound offers a safe, fun way to find Internet sites related to this book. All of the sites on FactHound have been researched by our staff. Here's all you do:

Visit *www.facthound.com*

FactHound will fetch the best sites for you!

INDEX